Things Boundaries are Allowed to Do

(An Incomplete List)

Ben Kucenski

I0520602

Things Boundaries are Allowed to Do

(An Incomplete List)

Paperback Edition: 979-8-9939525-1-2

Copyright © 2025 Ben Kucenski

Who Is My Neighbor?

The question is not new.

It appears early in the Bible and again at the very center of Jesus' teaching. It is asked by people who want clarity — and sometimes by people who want limits.

Who is my neighbor?

The question matters because it decides who we feel responsible for, who we notice, and who we can ignore.

In the Hebrew Scriptures, the idea of "neighbor" is already broader than comfort would suggest. The law commands care not only for family and community, but also for the stranger, the outsider, the one with no power to repay.

"You shall love the stranger, for you were strangers once."

Neighborliness is never confined to similarity. It is defined by proximity and vulnerability.

Still, people kept asking for boundaries.

So someone once asked Jesus directly, "Who is my neighbor?"

They were not asking because they didn't want to love. They were asking because they wanted to know **how far love had to go**.

Jesus answered the question the way he often did — with a story.

A man is beaten and left on the side of the road. Others pass by. Some are respected. Some are religious. Some are busy. Some have reasons.

Then someone stops — someone who was not expected to stop.

Jesus does not ask who caused the harm.
He does not ask whether the injured man made good choices.
He does not ask whether helping is complicated.

He asks a different question:

Who acted as a neighbor?

The answer is uncomfortable in its simplicity.

The neighbor is the one who saw vulnerability and chose care.

Not the one with the right position.
Not the one with the best intentions.
Not the one with authority.

The neighbor is the one who did not pass by.

And then Jesus says something that leaves no room for narrowing the definition:

"Go and do likewise."

He does not say, "Go and decide who deserves this."
He does not say, "Go and do this when it is convenient."
He does not say, "Go and do this only for those who are like you."

He makes neighbor-love an action, not a category.

Neighbor Is Not an Age Category

Nothing in Scripture suggests that children stop being neighbors because they are young.

Nothing suggests that teenagers stop being neighbors because they are developing.

Nothing suggests that vulnerability disqualifies someone from dignity.

If anything, Scripture moves in the opposite direction.

The younger, the weaker, the more dependent — the **greater** the responsibility of those with power.

Jesus does not treat children as interruptions or abstractions. He places them at the center.

"Whoever welcomes one such child in my name welcomes me."

This is not sentimental language. It is moral language.

To welcome someone is to make space for them.
To protect them.
To take responsibility for how your power affects them.

Children are not neighbors *in theory*.
They are neighbors **in practice**, precisely because they depend on adults.

Neighbor Is Not Limited by Comfort

In the very first pages of the Bible, after the first act of violence between humans, a question is asked that echoes through history:

"Am I my brother's keeper?"

The question is framed as deflection.
It is an attempt to avoid responsibility.

And the story answers it clearly.

Yes.

You are.

To be someone's keeper does not mean control.
It does not mean ownership.
It does not mean surveillance.

It means responsibility where your actions — or inaction — have consequences for another's safety.

You do not have to intend harm to be responsible for preventing it.

You do not have to cause suffering to be accountable for responding to it.

Scripture does not allow moral neutrality in the face of vulnerability.

All Humans, All Ages

When Jesus teaches love of neighbor, he does not attach qualifiers.

He does not say:

- "Only adults."

- "Only those who can speak clearly."

- "Only those who understand what's happening."

- "Only those who are strong enough to resist."

He speaks to *all humans*, because all humans bear God's image.

Age does not diminish that image.
Dependence does not weaken it.
Confusion does not erase it.

If anything, those realities increase the obligation of those with power.

Why This Matters for Boundaries

Boundaries are one of the primary ways we live out neighbor-love.

They are how people with power refuse to take advantage of it.
They are how care is made visible.
They are how love becomes practical.

Boundaries say:

- *Your safety matters more than my comfort.*

- *Your growth matters more than my access.*

- *Your dignity matters more than my desires.*

When we ask, "Who is my neighbor?" and take Scripture seriously, the answer is unavoidable.

Every person is your neighbor.
Every age.
Every stage.
Every level of vulnerability.

And love does not ask how close it can get without consequence.

Love asks how well it can protect.

Am I My Brother's Keeper?

The question appears very early in the Bible.

It is asked after harm has already been done.

After violence.
After denial.
After an attempt to disappear responsibility with words.

"Am I my brother's keeper?"

The question is not asked in confusion.
It is asked in defense.

It is the first attempt to claim moral neutrality.

What happened is tragic, but it's not my responsibility.

Scripture does not accept that answer.

It never argues with Cain directly.
It simply reveals that the question itself is wrong.

Yes — you are your brother's keeper.

Not because you control him.
Not because you own him.
But because you live in proximity to him, and your choices affect his life.

From the beginning, the Bible ties responsibility to
relationship and power, not to intent.

Keeping Is Not Controlling

To be a "keeper" does not mean watching every move.

It does not mean suspicion.
It does not mean surveillance.
It does not mean assuming guilt.

It means **taking responsibility for what happens when you have the ability to intervene**.

A keeper notices vulnerability.
A keeper refuses indifference.
A keeper does not ask, "Is this my job?" when harm is possible.

This is why the question appears so early.
Human beings have always tried to step away from responsibility by narrowing it.

Scripture refuses to let us do that.

The Good Samaritan as Keeper

When Jesus tells the story of the Good Samaritan, he is answering *two* questions at once.

He is answering:

- Who is my neighbor?

And he is answering:

- Am I my brother's keeper?

The beaten man on the road is clearly a neighbor — vulnerable, exposed, unable to protect himself.

But the Samaritan is doing something more than noticing.

He stops.
He interrupts his plans.
He uses his resources.
He puts his own body at risk.
He ensures ongoing care.

This is not accidental kindness.

This is **keeping**.

The Samaritan does not say:

- "I didn't cause this."

- "This isn't my responsibility."

- "Someone else will handle it."

- "I don't want to misunderstand the situation."

He understands something deeper:

When harm is possible, refusing responsibility is a moral choice.

Jesus makes this unavoidable by asking a final question:

"Which of these was a neighbor?"

Not:

- Who felt compassion?

- Who had good theology?

- Who avoided wrongdoing?

But:

- Who took responsibility?

And then Jesus says again:

"Go and do likewise."

Keeping Always Flows From Power

Scripture consistently assigns greater responsibility to those with greater power.

Parents are accountable for children.
Shepherds are accountable for flocks.
Leaders are accountable for communities.
Those who see danger are accountable for warning.

This is not because power is evil.
It is because power creates **impact**.

You do not need to intend harm for your actions to matter.
You do not need to be malicious to be responsible.

The Bible does not ask whether harm was intended.
It asks whether harm was **prevented**.

Children Make This Question Clearer, Not Harder

Children clarify moral responsibility because the imbalance is obvious.

They have:

- Less experience

- Less authority

- Less ability to leave

- Less ability to name harm

Adults have:

- Access

- Authority

- Control

- Credibility

In Scripture, this imbalance never reduces responsibility. It **increases** it.

That is why Jesus speaks so sharply about those who cause harm to the vulnerable.

That is why he places children in the center, not on the margins.

Being a keeper is not about reacting after harm occurs. It is about **structuring life so harm is less likely to occur at all**.

Boundaries Are the Language of Keeping

This is where boundaries enter the story.

Boundaries are not walls against love.
They are the shape love takes when power is involved.

Boundaries say:

- I will not put you in a position where you must protect yourself from me.

- I will not ask you to carry adult needs.

- I will not rely on secrecy.

- I will not test temptation.

- I will not assume trust is enough.

A person who refuses boundaries while claiming good intentions is not acting as a keeper.

A keeper does not ask how close they can get without crossing a line.

A keeper asks:

- What does this person need to be safe?

- What limits protect both of us?

- What choices remove pressure rather than create it?

No Neutral Ground

"Am I my brother's keeper?" is not a philosophical question.

It is a moral dividing line.

Scripture answers it consistently:

- When you have power, you have responsibility.

- When you see vulnerability, you have obligation.

- When harm is possible, inaction is a choice.

The Good Samaritan does not merely prove who the neighbor is.

He shows what a keeper looks like.

He does not fix everything.
He does not control the injured man's future.
He does not claim ownership.

He does what he can — and ensures care continues.

That is keeping.

Why This Comes Before the List

Before we talk about what boundaries are allowed to do, we need to know **why they exist at all**.

Boundaries are not about fear.
They are not about suspicion.
They are not about punishment.

They are about answering two ancient questions honestly:

Who is my neighbor?
Am I my brother's keeper?

If the answer to both is *yes*, then boundaries are not optional.

They are love made concrete.

What Is a Boundary?

Before we talk about what boundaries are allowed to do, we need to be clear about what a boundary **is**.

A boundary is **not** something you put around other people.

A boundary is something you put **around yourself**.

That distinction matters.

A Boundary Is Not a Weapon

Boundaries are often misunderstood because they are confused with control.

A boundary does not say:

- *You must behave this way.*

- *You are not allowed to feel this.*

- *You have to change so I'm comfortable.*

Those are rules for others.
Those are demands.
Those are attempts to manage someone else's choices.

That is not a boundary.

A boundary says something different:

- *This is what I will do.*

- *This is what I will not do.*

- *This is where I will step back.*

- *This is how I will keep myself — and others — safe.*

Boundaries do not reach outward to restrain.
They reach inward to clarify responsibility.

Walls Are Not Always Bad

When people hear the word "wall," they often think of fear, isolation, or rejection.

But Scripture does not treat walls that way.

Walls protect what is vulnerable.
Walls mark responsibility.
Walls make it clear where care must be intentional.

A city without walls is described as unsafe — not virtuous.

In the same way, a person without boundaries is not more loving.
They are simply more exposed.

A boundary is a wall that says:

- *Here is where my responsibility begins.*

- *Here is where it ends.*

That clarity is not unkind.
It is honest.

Boundaries Protect Relationship — Not Just Individuals

This is where boundaries are often misunderstood.

People assume boundaries are about distance.

But healthy boundaries actually **make relationship possible**.

Without boundaries:

- Power goes unchecked
- Confusion grows
- Expectations blur
- Harm becomes easier to excuse

Boundaries prevent relationships from becoming places where:

- One person carries more than they should
- Another person avoids responsibility
- Silence replaces clarity

A boundary does not end connection.
It **defines the terms under which connection is safe**.

Boundaries Are How Keepers Act

This connects directly back to the Good Samaritan.

The Samaritan does not take control of the injured man's life.
He does not stay forever.
He does not demand gratitude.

He does what is his to do — and no more.

That is a boundary.

Being a keeper does not mean unlimited access.
It means appropriate responsibility.

Boundaries are how people with power prevent their power
from becoming harm.

You Can Only Place a Boundary on Yourself

This is one of the most important truths in this book.

You cannot place a boundary on someone else.

You can:

- Ask
- Invite
- Explain
- Request

But a boundary is always about **your own action**.

For example:

- *I will only meet in public spaces.*
- *I will include others in communication.*
- *I will not keep secrets that affect safety.*
- *I will step away if this becomes unsafe.*

These statements do not control others.
They clarify what *you* will do.

That clarity is protective — especially for children and vulnerable people.

Boundaries Are Not Accusations

Another reason boundaries are resisted is because people hear them as judgments.

But boundaries do not say:

- *You are dangerous.*

- *You are untrustworthy.*

- *You have bad intentions.*

They say:

- *I take responsibility for my role.*

- *I do not rely on good intentions alone.*

- *I value safety more than convenience.*

Good boundaries assume neither guilt nor innocence. They assume **human limitation**.

And Scripture is very realistic about human limitation.

Why Boundaries Matter Before Harm Happens

Boundaries are most powerful **before** something goes wrong.

They prevent:

- Pressure
- Ambiguity
- Special exceptions
- Gradual erosion of safety

A boundary does not wait until someone is uncomfortable enough to speak.

It removes the need for that discomfort in the first place.

That is why boundaries are not signs of distrust.
They are signs of wisdom.

This Is What We Mean Going Forward

When this book talks about boundaries, it means:

- Walls you place around *yourself*
- Choices that limit *your own* behavior
- Structures that reduce risk
- Practices that protect the vulnerable
- Clarity that removes pressure

Not punishment.
Not suspicion.
Not control.

Boundaries are allowed to exist because people matter.

And when power is involved, love without boundaries is not love at all.

A Boundary in Motion: Square Dancing

One way to understand a boundary is to see it **in action**.

Square dancing gives us a surprisingly clear example.

In many forms of square dancing, men extend a hand. They do not grab.

The hand is offered as a **support**.

Women are free to place their hand on that support in whatever way feels comfortable to them — lightly, firmly, briefly, or not at all.

The boundary is clear:

- The man offers space.

- The woman chooses contact.

That choice belongs entirely to her.

The Boundary Is the Support

The extended hand is not a grip.
It is not a hook.
It is not a command.

It is a stable surface that says:

You may engage here if you wish.

The man's responsibility is not to hold the woman.
It is to **support her movement without controlling it**.

That is what a boundary looks like when it is working.

What Happens When the Boundary Is Violated

Sometimes, a man grips instead of offering a support.

This is not usually dramatic.
It is not overtly violent.
It does not look shocking from across the room.

But everyone understands something immediately:

That is not a safe dancer.

Why?

Because gripping removes choice.

It turns guidance into control.
It replaces consent with assumption.
It signals that the man believes access is his once contact begins.

Even when the harm is small, the meaning is clear.

A person who grips where a platform is expected does not understand — or does not respect — the boundary.

Guidance Without Control

In square dancing, the support has another important function.

It guides — but it does not force.

If the man moves slightly off direction, the woman often continues where she is supposed to go **without him**.

The dance still works.

Why?

Because the boundary was never about domination.
It was about **coordination**.

The structure allows both dancers to move freely while staying connected.

That is the goal of a boundary.

Why This Matters

This example shows something essential:

Boundaries are not about stopping movement.
They are about **making movement safe**.

A boundary:

- Offers support without pressure

- Creates connection without control

- Allows choice without confusion

- Makes harm noticeable without drama

When someone violates a small, well-understood boundary, people don't say,
"That person is evil."

They say,
"That person is not safe."

That distinction matters.

Consent Is Often Quiet

Square dancing shows us something else that is important to understand.

Consent does not always look like a spoken agreement.

Often, it looks like:

- An offered hand

- A chosen response

- A mutual understanding of roles

- Respect for limits

When that understanding is broken, people don't need a lecture to recognize it.

They feel it.

Boundaries make safety visible.

Boundaries Are About Responsibility

The man does not need to decide how the woman should hold his hand.

He does not need to test her comfort.
He does not need to "lead harder."

His responsibility is simple:

- Offer the platform

- Maintain it

- Release when the movement ends

That is a boundary placed **around his own behavior**.

The woman's responsibility is different:

- Choose how to engage

- Follow the dance as she understands it

- Let go when she needs to

Neither controls the other.

That is what consent looks like in motion.

This Is Why Boundaries Matter

Boundaries are not always dramatic.

Often, they are subtle, learned, and widely understood.

And when someone ignores them, even slightly, people notice — because boundaries are how safety is communicated.

This is why boundaries do not have to accuse.

They simply have to exist.

What It Means to Be "Not Safe"

In the square dance, something important is already doing a lot of work.

Everything happens **in public**.

The caller can see every movement.
Other dancers can see every interaction.
Nothing is hidden.
Nothing is rushed.
Nothing depends on private interpretation.

This matters more than people realize.

Safety is not only about who people are.

It is about **where things happen, how they happen**, and **who can see**.

Safety Is Built Into the Space

A square dance is designed to limit risk.

- The space is open.

- The rules are shared.

- The instructions are external.

- The purpose is clear.

- The time is defined.

- The beginning and end are obvious.

There are no drinks to lower inhibitions.
There are no side conversations that matter more than the dance.
There is no expectation of intimacy.
There is no reward for secrecy.

Everyone is there to do the same thing, together, in the same way.

That structure doesn't make people virtuous.
It makes harm **harder**.

Visibility Inhibits Gross Misconduct

When everyone can see what is happening, boundaries matter more.

Small violations are noticeable.
Patterns become visible.
Discomfort is easier to trust.

If someone grips instead of offering a platform, others see it.

No one needs to shout.
No one needs to accuse.
No one needs to panic.

People simply understand:
That person is not safe to dance with.

And because the space is public and structured, that understanding can be acted on calmly.

What "Not Safe" Means Here

"Not safe" does not mean:

- Evil

- Dangerous in every context

- Beyond redemption

It means something simpler and more precise:

This person does not respect the boundaries that make this space work.

Because of that, **their access does not expand**.

Safety Is About Limiting Expansion

In a healthy system, unsafe behavior does not lead to escalation.

It leads to **containment**.

Someone who violates boundaries:

- Is not invited into smaller spaces
- Is not given more access
- Is not given privacy
- Is not given exceptions
- Is not given situations that reduce inhibitions

Nothing dramatic needs to happen.

The boundary simply holds.

The Power of the Large Public Space

The dance begins and ends in the same public place.

There is no pressure to continue elsewhere.
No expectation of a "next step."
No drifting into quieter, more private settings.

You say "thank you."
You let go.
You return to the group.

And that is enough.

When boundaries are clear, **leaving does not require explanation**.

Saying No Inside the Boundary

One of the most important things about a safe space is this:

It makes saying "no" easy.

You don't have to invent a reason.
You don't have to justify discomfort.
You don't have to manage someone else's feelings.

The structure does the work for you.

You can say no **without confrontation**, because the boundary already exists.

That is what safety looks like.

Why This Matters Beyond the Dance

Most harm does not begin with dramatic violations.

It begins when:

- Visibility decreases

- Structure loosens

- Inhibitions are lowered

- Expectations become personal

- Boundaries blur

- Isolation increases

Healthy systems notice early signals and **do not expand access** in response.

They don't ask:
How do we smooth this over?

They ask:
How do we keep this contained?

Safety Is Not Punishment

When someone is not safe, limiting access is not punishment.

It is stewardship.

It protects:

- The vulnerable
- The community
- The integrity of the space
- Even the person whose behavior is limited

Boundaries do not announce judgment.

They quietly prevent harm.

This Is What Boundaries Do

Boundaries:

- Keep things visible

- Prevent isolation

- Reduce pressure

- Make "no" possible

- Stop harm before it escalates

They do not require fear.
They do not require suspicion.
They require clarity.

And when boundaries are clear, safety becomes something people can feel   not something they have to argue for.

Safety Is Sometimes Person-Specific

When we talk about someone being "not safe," it's important to be precise.

"Not safe" is not always a universal judgment about who a person is.

Sometimes it is a statement about **fit**.

In square dancing, different people enjoy different styles of movement.

Some dancers prefer light contact and clear space.
Others enjoy strong momentum, dramatic turns, or being guided more forcefully.

Neither preference is wrong.

What matters is **mutual understanding and consent**.

Why We Don't Rush to Moral Judgment

This is why healthy systems don't immediately turn every boundary mismatch into a crisis.

If one dancer grips when another expects a platform, the issue may not be malice.
It may be incompatibility.

That dancer might be perfectly acceptable — even welcome — to someone who enjoys that style.

The problem is not that the person exists.
The problem is that **this pairing doesn't work**.

So the solution is not punishment.

The solution is **choice**.

Choice Is a Safety Tool

In a healthy space, people can switch partners.

They can step back.
They can rejoin the group.
They can choose a different interaction.

That freedom matters.

It means no one has to endure discomfort just to avoid conflict.
It means no one has to decide whether something is "bad enough" to justify leaving.
It means safety can be maintained without confrontation.

Choice allows boundaries to function quietly.

Being Unsafe for Me Is Still Enough

This is a crucial point.

Someone does not need to be unsafe *for everyone* to be unsafe *for you*.

Your boundary does not require consensus.

If a person's behavior:

- Feels wrong to you

- Removes your sense of choice

- Makes you brace instead of relax

- Pushes beyond what you want

That is sufficient.

You do not owe anyone an explanation beyond your boundary.

We Become Safe by Staying Inside Our Boundaries

Safety does not require fixing other people.

It does not require diagnosing intentions.
It does not require public judgment.

You become safer by:

- Staying in visible spaces

- Choosing compatible partners

- Ending interactions cleanly

- Returning to the group

- Letting boundaries do their work

You can remain safe **even when someone else is not safe for you**, as long as the system allows choice and visibility.

Why This Distinction Matters

This distinction prevents two common mistakes:

1. **Overreaction**
   Treating every mismatch as moral failure or danger

2. **Underreaction**
   Telling yourself discomfort doesn't count unless everyone agrees

Healthy boundaries avoid both.

They allow people to sort themselves naturally — without shame, secrecy, or escalation.

Avoidance is not a boundary, it just allows behaviors to continue.

Boundaries Are About Fit, Not Force

A boundary does not say:

- *You are bad.*

It says:

- *This doesn't work for me.*

That sentence is enough.

And when systems are designed well — like the square dance — that sentence doesn't have to be spoken out loud.

The structure already supports it.

This Is Another Way Boundaries Keep Us Safe

Boundaries:

- Allow differences without conflict
- Prevent pressure to endure discomfort
- Make exit normal
- Reduce the need for confrontation
- Keep people from being trapped in mismatches

They do not demand agreement.

They protect choice.

When Preference Becomes Pressure

Up to now, the square dance has shown us how boundaries work when everyone respects choice.

But sometimes something changes.

Sometimes the dancer who grips does not simply prefer that style.
They **target** someone.

They seek the same partner again and again.
They insist their way of dancing is the *right* way.
They frame discomfort as misunderstanding.
They treat consent as something to be negotiated rather than honored.

And when the other dancer objects, they complain.

When a Boundary Is Reframed as a Problem

This is an important moment.

The issue is no longer about compatibility.
It is no longer about different styles.

It becomes about **projection**.

The gripping dancer begins to act as though:

- Their preference should determine the other person's comfort

- Their experience should override the other person's body

- Their intention should outweigh the other person's response

They may say things like:

- *You're overreacting.*

- *This is how it's supposed to work.*

- *You just need to relax.*

- *No one else has a problem with this.*

What they are really saying is:
My desire should define your boundary.

That is no longer a mismatch.

That is pressure.

Why This Changes the Safety Equation

At this point, the problem is not the grip.

The problem is **insistence**.

A safe person notices resistance and adjusts.
An unsafe person notices resistance and argues.

A safe person accepts "no" as information.
An unsafe person treats "no" as something to overcome.

This is why earlier we said that boundaries are walls you place around yourself.

The moment someone tries to move that wall for you, the issue is no longer style.

It is control.

"Shocked" Is Not the Same as Innocent

Often, people who project their desires onto others are genuinely surprised when it goes wrong.

They may say — or feel —

- *I didn't mean anything by it.*

- *I thought they liked it.*

- *I was just being friendly.*

- *I don't understand why this is a big deal.*

This shock is not proof of safety.

It is often proof that they were paying more attention to their own experience than to the other person's response.

Being surprised that someone does not want what you want is not the same as being attentive.

When Complaints Replace Curiosity

There is a clear signal that a boundary has crossed into unsafety:

When someone complains **about** a boundary instead of respecting it.

At that point:

- The structure is no longer protecting the vulnerable
- Choice is being reframed as rejection
- Discomfort is being treated as an inconvenience
- The person who spoke up is subtly blamed

This is where systems matter.

Healthy systems do not debate someone's discomfort.
They do not ask the vulnerable person to justify themselves.
They do not reward persistence.

They simply **hold the boundary**.

Why This Allegory Matters

The square dance example is small and ordinary — and that's the point.

Most harm does not begin with dramatic violations.
It begins with someone assuming their desire should be shared, and reacting poorly when it isn't.

Projection turns preference into entitlement.
Entitlement turns contact into pressure.
Pressure turns boundaries into obstacles.

And when boundaries are treated as obstacles, safety erodes quickly.

This Is the Line We Were Drawing All Along

Earlier, we said:

- Safety can be person-specific
- Not every mismatch requires escalation
- Choice and visibility can resolve many situations

All of that remains true.

But when someone:

- Targets rather than accepts chance
- Insists rather than adjusts
- Argues rather than listens
- Complains rather than steps back

The situation has changed.

This is no longer about dancing.

It is about **who believes they get to decide**.

Why Boundaries Must Hold

Boundaries exist for moments like this.

They protect people from having to argue for their own limits.
They prevent desire from becoming dominance.
They make it possible to disengage without explanation.

And they remind everyone of something essential:

No one owes anyone reciprocity.

Not in dancing.
Not in conversation.
Not in attention.
Not in affection.

When that truth is honored, safety is possible.

When it is not, boundaries are no longer optional.

They are necessary.

Boundaries in Mutual Dating

So far, our examples have involved clear roles and visible spaces.

But boundaries also matter when two people are close in age, mutually interested, and choosing to spend time together.

This is where things often feel less clear — not because boundaries disappear, but because **communication changes.**

When People Don't Say Everything Out Loud

In dating, people don't usually spell out exactly what they're comfortable with.

Not because they're being deceptive — but because:

- It can feel awkward

- It can feel unromantic

- It can feel risky

- It can feel like saying the quiet part out loud

Most people don't say:

"I am comfortable holding hands but not kissing."
"I would like to stop here."
"I don't want this to go further tonight."

Instead, people communicate through **pace, posture, and response**.

This is normal.

The Game of Escalation

Because people don't state everything explicitly, dating often becomes a quiet game of escalation.

One person leans a little closer.
The other responds — or doesn't.

One person reaches for a hand.
The other either accepts, shifts away, or lets go.

Each step is a question:
Is this okay?

Each response is an answer.

Escalation is not automatically bad.
It can be mutual, careful, and respectful.

The problem begins when **responses are ignored**.

How Escalation Becomes Pressure

Escalation stops being mutual when:

- One person keeps advancing after hesitation
- Silence is treated as consent
- Stillness is treated as agreement
- Discomfort is brushed aside
- Momentum replaces attention

At that point, escalation is no longer a shared dance.

It becomes a push.

And pushes don't feel romantic — even when attraction exists.

How to Stop Escalation

Stopping escalation does not require confrontation.

It can be as simple as:

- Pulling back
- Changing position
- Creating space
- Standing up
- Ending the activity
- Saying "not tonight"
- Saying "I'd like to slow down"

None of these are rude.
None of these are betrayals.

They are **boundaries in motion**.

What Respect Actually Looks Like

This is a crucial truth:

If someone likes you, they will respect your boundary.

Not grudgingly.
Not resentfully.
Not with pressure.
Not with disappointment turned into guilt.

They will:

- Pause

- Adjust

- Accept the answer

- End the date kindly

- Leave you feeling safe, not ashamed

A respectful ending is a sign of genuine interest — not its absence.

Why Ending Well Matters

How a date ends tells you more than how it begins.

Someone who:

- Becomes cold
- Acts wounded
- Makes you feel guilty
- Suggests you "led them on"
- Pushes for "just a little more"

is telling you something important.

They are not responding to your boundary —
they are responding to their own frustration.

That is information.

Mutual Interest Includes Mutual Care

Healthy dating is not about how far things go.

It's about how carefully people pay attention to each other.

Mutual interest means:

- No one is rushed

- No one is tested

- No one has to prove anything

- No one has to override discomfort to be liked

You don't owe escalation to maintain connection.

You don't owe explanation to maintain dignity.

Boundaries Protect Attraction

This may sound surprising, but boundaries do not ruin romance.

They protect it.

They prevent resentment.
They prevent confusion.
They prevent regret.
They allow trust to grow instead of pressure.

A person who respects your boundary today is more likely to be safe tomorrow.

A person who resents your boundary today is already telling you how they handle "no."

Ending on a Positive Note

Stopping escalation does not mean ending connection.

It means choosing to end the moment **well**.

A healthy ending looks like:

- Kindness

- Warmth

- Clarity

- Respect

- Space to breathe

That is not rejection.

That is care.

This Is Still the Same Boundary

Just like the square dance:

- Guidance without grip
- Movement without force
- Choice without pressure
- Visibility without exposure

Dating is still a dance of consent.

When both people are paying attention, it works.

When one person insists on leading past comfort, it stops being a dance.

And that is when boundaries matter most.

Long-Term Relationship vs. Short-Term Manipulation

Before we talk about preventing trauma, it helps to talk about **time**.

Because many boundary violations don't come from cruelty. They come from anxiety.

"Will You Still Love Me Tomorrow?"

That question has been asked for a long time.

It's not really about love.
It's about fear.

It's the fear that:

- This moment is all there is

- This night must decide everything

- If something doesn't happen now, it may never happen

- If I don't give in, I will lose them

That fear changes how people behave.

When Relationships Feel Like They're Flailing

In a flailing relationship, nothing feels secure.

People don't know:

- Where they stand
- When they'll see each other again
- Whether interest will last
- Whether affection must be proven

So pressure builds.

Not always spoken pressure — often internal.

If I don't say yes now, maybe there won't be another chance.

That's how people end up doing things they weren't ready for — not because they wanted to, but because they were afraid of losing connection.

That's not intimacy.

That's anxiety making decisions.

Short-Term Thinking Creates Pressure

Short-term thinking says:

- *Everything has to happen tonight.*

- *This moment is fragile.*

- *We can't slow down.*

- *If we stop, it might disappear.*

That mindset turns affection into urgency.

Urgency is not romance.
Urgency is not care.
Urgency is not trust.

Urgency is a warning sign.

Long-Term Thinking Changes Everything

A long-term relationship thinks differently.

It says:

- *We don't have to do everything at once.*

- *This isn't a race.*

- *Time together is the point.*

- *Being here matters more than what happens.*

Or, as we could summarize:

*"We don't have to do everything in one night.
This isn't a Christmas Carol."*

Nothing has to be redeemed before midnight.

Calming the Anxious Brain With Time

One of the kindest things people can do — especially for themselves — is **think in months instead of moments.**

Ask:

- *What would this feel like in three months?*

- *What would safety look like in six months?*

- *Would I feel cared for if nothing changed tonight?*

Time calms the nervous system.

Time reminds us:

- We are not being chased

- We are not being tested

- We are not running out of chances

When time is real, pressure fades.

In a Relationship, Presence Is the Thing

This matters especially for younger teenagers.

At that stage of life:

- Brains are still developing

- Emotions are intense

- Attachment feels urgent

- Loss feels catastrophic

Which is why presence matters more than escalation.

Being together.
Being supported.
Being seen.
Being allowed to exist without performing.

Those things build safety.

Physical escalation does not create connection —
connection creates safety, and safety determines what comes next.

Manipulation Always Rushes the Timeline

One of the clearest signs of manipulation is **speed**.

Manipulation says:

- *If you cared, you would...*
- *This is what couples do.*
- *Everyone else is doing this.*
- *Why are you making this difficult?*

Manipulation collapses the future into the present.

It needs urgency because it can't survive patience.

A relationship that cannot wait is telling you something important.

Long-Term Care Looks Boring From the Outside

Healthy relationships often look boring to outsiders.

They include:

- Sitting together
- Talking
- Shared routines
- Predictable time
- Reassurance
- Consistency

But that "boring" is actually stability.

And stability is what allows intimacy to be chosen — not forced.

You Don't Prove Love by Giving In

This is worth saying plainly:

You do not prove love by overriding your comfort.
You do not prove commitment by escalating.
You do not prove maturity by rushing.

Love that lasts is not afraid of tomorrow.

If someone cares about you, they will want you to feel safe
over time, not overwhelmed in a moment.

Time Is a Boundary, Too

Thinking in months is a boundary.

Ending a date kindly is a boundary.
Saying "not tonight" is a boundary.
Choosing presence over pressure is a boundary.

These boundaries don't stop relationships.

They protect them.

Especially for Younger Teens

For younger teenagers especially, this matters:

You are not behind.
You are not late.
You are not missing your chance.

A relationship where:

- Someone shows up
- Someone listens
- Someone waits
- Someone respects pace

is already a good relationship.

That is enough.

Where This Leads Next

Understanding the difference between long-term care and short-term pressure helps us see why boundaries matter **before harm happens**.

Because trauma doesn't usually begin with violence.

It begins when time is taken away.

Next, we'll talk about how boundaries protect people when pressure appears — and how to recognize when something is no longer about connection, but about control.

Manipulation Through Space and Substances

Some forms of manipulation don't look like pressure at first.

They look like convenience.
They look like generosity.
They look like romance.

But what they actually do is **change the conditions under which decisions are made**.

And that matters.

Space Changes Power

Where something happens affects how safe it is.

Public spaces:

- Keep things visible

- Allow easy exit

- Reduce pressure

- Invite accountability

Private spaces do the opposite.

That doesn't mean private spaces are always unsafe.
It means they **increase responsibility**.

Because once you are alone with someone, the balance of power changes — even if the person is kind, even if you like them, even if nothing bad is intended.

That's why the timing of the move into private space matters.

A Healthy Decision Is Made Before You Go Home

In a healthy relationship, the decision to go home with someone is made **before** anything else changes.

It is made:

- In public
- While sober
- Without urgency
- Without secrecy

You know where you are going.
You know who you are with.
You know how to leave.

Your friends know:

- His name
- His address
- That you are going with him

They may even:

- Have his phone number
- Be connected to him on social media
- Know his friends or family

Nothing about the decision is hidden.

That visibility is not about distrust.
It is about **safety being shared**.

Connection Makes Safety Feel Real

One reason healthy situations feel safe is because they are **connected**.

You are not disappearing into someone else's world.
You are stepping into a space that is linked to your own.

You can:

- Text someone

- Leave if you need to

- Be found

- Be remembered

When you imagine going home with him, it feels safe — not because you expect nothing to happen, but because **nothing is being rushed or concealed**.

You might feel a little anxious about what you plan to do there.

That's normal.

Anxiety about intimacy is not the same as fear about safety.

Alcohol and other Drugs Change the Order of Things

This is where manipulation often enters.

Alcohol changes how people feel, think, and decide.

That's not a moral statement.
It's a physical one.

Alcohol:

- Lowers inhibitions
- Blurs judgment
- Makes it harder to read discomfort
- Makes it harder to act on hesitation

Because of that, **the order matters**.

Drinks Are for After the Decision

In a healthy situation:

- The decision is made first
- The boundaries are clear
- The destination is known
- The option to leave is real

Drinks come **after**.

Alcohol is not used to:

- Make the decision feel easier
- Quiet doubt
- Push past hesitation
- Take down boundaries

When substances are introduced *before* clarity, they are not neutral.

They are shaping consent.

When Alcohol Becomes a Tool

It's a warning sign when:

- Going somewhere private depends on drinking
- Hesitation is met with "just relax"
- Boundaries are framed as nerves to be overcome
- Sobriety is treated as an obstacle

That doesn't mean harm is inevitable.

It means the situation is being structured in a way that **reduces choice**.

Healthy people don't need reduced choice to feel close.

Safety Is About Sequence

This is the simplest way to think about it:

Healthy sequence:

1. Interest

2. Clarity

3. Decision

4. Privacy

5. Optional substances

Unhealthy sequence:

1. Substances

2. Isolation

3. Pressure

4. Confusion

5. Regret

The difference is not attraction.

It's **order**.

You Are Allowed to Keep Your Boundaries Intact

You are allowed to say:

- "I want to decide this sober."

- "Let's wait."

- "I don't want drinks right now."

- "I'm not ready to go somewhere private."

Anyone who respects you will respect that.

Anyone who needs your boundaries lowered to proceed is telling you something important.

Safety Is Not the Absence of Desire

It's important to say this clearly:

Wanting someone does not mean you owe them access.
Feeling curious does not mean you have to act.
Being attracted does not erase your right to decide slowly.

Safety is not about killing desire.

It's about making sure desire is **chosen**, not engineered.

This Is Still About Boundaries

Just like the square dance:

- Visibility matters
- Structure matters
- Sequence matters
- Choice matters

Boundaries are allowed to say:

- *Not like this.*
- *Not yet.*
- *Not this way.*

And when boundaries are respected, connection doesn't disappear.

It gets stronger.

Why This Comes Before Trauma

Most trauma does not begin with force.

It begins when:

- Space shrinks
- Inhibitions drop
- Pressure increases
- Exit options fade

Understanding how manipulation uses space and substances helps people protect themselves **before harm occurs**.

Which is exactly what boundaries are for.

The Sex Pest: When Interest Becomes Transactional

There is a particular pattern that shows up often enough to deserve a name.

Not because it is rare.
But because it is **predictable**.

It's the person who believes that time, effort, or niceness should eventually be **paid back** with access.

"I've Put in My Time"

This person often describes themselves as a "nice guy."

They:

- Text regularly

- Listen patiently

- Show up

- Offer help

- Wait "respectfully"

At first, nothing looks wrong.

The problem isn't kindness.
The problem is **accounting**.

They are not relating — they are **accumulating credit**.

And eventually, they expect to cash it in.

When Care Has a Price Tag

Transactional thinking sounds like:

- *After everything I've done...*

- *I've been patient long enough.*

- *I waited for you.*

- *You owe me a chance.*

- *This is what relationships do.*

- *Don't I deserve something?*

Notice what's missing.

There is no curiosity about your comfort.
No interest in your pace.
No respect for your boundaries as real answers.

There is only frustration that the transaction is not completing.

Persistence After "No" Is the Red Flag

This matters:

Interest that continues after a clear boundary is no longer interest.

It is entitlement.

A relational person hears "no" as information.
A transactional person hears "no" as a delay.

They don't stop.
They negotiate.

They push gently.
Then less gently.

They frame persistence as romance.

The Illusion of Choice

Transactional people often say:

- *I'm not forcing you.*

- *It's your decision.*

- *I just want you to think about it.*

But if your "choice" comes with:

- Repeated pressure

- Guilt

- Withdrawal of kindness

- Sulking

- Anger

- Accusations of being unfair or cold

Then it is not a free choice.

It is coercion dressed up as patience.

Why This Is Not About Being "Too Nice"

It's important to be clear.

This is not about:

- Shy people
- Awkward people
- People who feel disappointed
- People who are learning how to date

Feeling hurt is human.

What matters is **what someone does with that hurt**.

A safe person manages disappointment without turning it into pressure.

An unsafe person uses disappointment as leverage.

Relational vs. Transactional

Here is the difference in one sentence:

Relational people want mutual desire.
Transactional people want return on investment.

Relational people ask:

- *Do you want this?*

- *Are you comfortable?*

- *Is this working for you?*

Transactional people ask:

- *When do I get something?*

- *How long do I have to wait?*

- *What did all that effort buy me?*

One treats you as a person.
The other treats you as a payoff.

The "Nice Guy" Mask Slips Under Frustration

One of the clearest indicators of this pattern is **what happens when you hold a boundary**.

A relational person:

- Respects it

- Adjusts

- Remains kind

- Ends things cleanly if needed

A transactional person:

- Becomes resentful

- Withdraws kindness

- Turns cold

- Complains

- Attacks your character

- Accuses you of using them

That shift tells you the kindness was conditional.

You Don't Owe Closure to Pressure

This is important to say plainly:

You do not owe continued access to someone who won't respect your boundaries.

You do not owe:

- More chances
- More explanations
- More patience
- Emotional caretaking

You are allowed to disengage when pressure appears.

Ending contact is not cruelty.
It is **self-protection**.

Why This Pattern Is So Dangerous

This pattern escalates because it **normalizes entitlement**.

Each step feels small:

- One more conversation

- One more chance

- One more explanation

- One more compromise

But the underlying belief never changes:
If I stay long enough, I will get what I want.

That belief does not coexist with consent.

Boundaries Are the Only Language This Pattern Understands

You cannot reason someone out of entitlement.

You cannot explain your way into being respected.

Boundaries are not punishment.
They are clarity.

And clarity ends transactions.

This Is Not About Gender — But It Is About Power

While this pattern is common among men socialized to believe persistence is romantic, the core issue is not masculinity.

It is **power without accountability**.

Anyone who treats connection as something to be earned and redeemed rather than shared and chosen is unsafe.

What To Notice Going Forward

Red flags are not dramatic.

They are consistent.

- Pressure after "no"
- Frustration at your pace
- Kindness that disappears when denied
- Attention that becomes resentment
- Effort that demands repayment

These are not misunderstandings.

They are information.

Why This Belongs Here

This chapter comes before trauma prevention for a reason.

Because trauma often begins when pressure is normalized.

Naming transactional behavior early helps people step away **before harm happens**.

Boundaries are allowed to stop persistence.

Boundaries are allowed to end access.

Boundaries are allowed to say:
I am not a transaction.

Avoiding Trauma

A comedian once asked a simple question.

She asked men:
What's the worst thing that could happen on a date?

They said things like:

- *Spill a drink on your shirt.*

- *Say something awkward.*

- *Get rejected.*

Then she asked women the same question.

Their answer:
Get murdered.

That gap matters.

Different Risks, Same World

This is not about fearmongering.
It is about reality.

Most dates do not end in violence.
Most people are not dangerous.

And still — the consequences of misjudgment are not evenly distributed.

That doesn't mean women are fragile.
It means the **cost of being wrong is higher**.

Acknowledging that is not paranoia.
It is awareness.

Boundaries Reduce Imagined "Debt"

One of the quiet ways boundaries help is by reducing what someone *thinks* you owe them.

Clear boundaries say:

- *This is not a misunderstanding.*

- *This was never on the table.*

- *There is no transaction in progress.*

When boundaries are stated and held early, there is less room for:

- *You led me on.*

- *You wasted my time.*

- *I thought this was going somewhere.*

Clarity collapses fantasy.

And fantasy is often where resentment grows.

"Why Are You Mad?"

Sometimes boundaries do their job perfectly.

When someone reacts to a boundary with irritation, agitation, or hostility, the boundary has revealed something important.

Not:

- *This person is evil.*

But:

- *This person is not regulating their emotions well.*

That information matters.

The sooner you see agitation, the sooner you can leave.

Early exits save energy.
Early exits reduce exposure.
Early exits reduce risk.

Getting Out Is a Skill, Not a Failure

Avoiding trauma is often about **leaving early**, not enduring well.

You do not need to:

- Calm someone down
- Teach them
- Give closure
- Make them feel understood
- Wait for proof

Discomfort is enough.

Agitation is enough.

A change in tone is enough.

Leaving is not rudeness.
Leaving is risk management.

Boundaries Are About Probability, Not Control

This part matters deeply:

Boundaries do not guarantee safety.

Some people escalate without warning.
Some people react violently to the first "no."
Some people go from calm to catastrophic in seconds.

Women have been punched for refusing a drink.
Women have been attacked for declining a phone number.
Women have been harmed without any chance to "do it right."

No boundary can stop that.

And none of this is a failure of the person who was harmed.

Improving Odds Is Not Blame

This must be said clearly.

What you do to protect yourself:

- Does not excuse violence
- Does not justify harm
- Does not transfer responsibility
- Does not mean you caused what happened

Responsibility always belongs to the person who chose to harm.

Full stop.

Risk awareness is not moral responsibility.

Why We Still Talk About Boundaries

So why talk about boundaries at all?

Because while boundaries can't eliminate danger, they can:

- Reduce exposure
- Reveal entitlement early
- Prevent escalation through ambiguity
- Create clean exits
- Increase visibility
- Limit isolation

They don't make you safe.

They make you **safer**.

That distinction matters.

Trauma Is Not Caused by "Doing It Wrong"

Trauma is not caused by:

- Being polite
- Being trusting
- Being hopeful
- Being kind
- Being curious

Trauma is caused by **violence and coercion**.

Boundaries are tools — not tests.

They exist to support you, not to judge you.

The Goal Is Not Fear

The goal is not to live afraid.

The goal is to live **clear**.

Clear about what you want.
Clear about what you don't.
Clear about when to leave.
Clear about whose reactions are not yours to manage.

Clarity does not guarantee safety.

But it improves your odds — and it preserves your dignity.

What Comes Next

Avoiding trauma is not about perfect decisions.

It's about:

- Seeing pressure early

- Trusting your discomfort

- Leaving when something shifts

- Holding boundaries without apology

- Knowing that none of this makes you responsible for someone else's violence

Next, we'll talk about what to do **when boundaries are ignored**, and how to protect yourself — emotionally and physically — when risk increases.

Because boundaries are allowed to be about survival.

And survival is not something anyone should have to justify.

When Boundaries Are Ignored

Most boundaries work.

They clarify expectations.
They slow things down.
They reveal who is safe.

But sometimes a boundary is ignored.

When that happens, the priority shifts.

It is no longer about politeness, explanation, or mutual understanding.

It is about **getting safe**.

When It Starts Small

Sometimes the first sign is simple:

- Someone won't stop touching you
- They keep putting their hand back
- They ignore pulling away
- They laugh it off
- They say "come on" or "relax"

At this point, you do not need to negotiate.

You do not need to soften your answer.

You do not need to explain why.

This is where action matters.

Get Out of the Situation

If you are on a date and someone will not respect physical boundaries:

- Call a cab

- Order a rideshare

- Leave the room

- Step outside

- Go back to a public space

- Call a friend

- Ask for help from staff if you are in a bar or restaurant

You are not required to manage their feelings.

You are not required to wait for the "right moment."

Leaving is enough.

If You Feel Unsafe, Trust That

You do not need certainty.

You do not need proof.

You do not need consensus.

Feeling unsafe is sufficient reason to leave.

The goal is not to determine whether something "counts."

The goal is to **stop exposure**.

When Someone Prevents You From Leaving

If someone:

- Blocks the door

- Takes your phone

- Refuses to let you leave

- Physically restrains you

- Escalates when you say no

This is no longer a boundary issue.

This is danger.

Your safety matters more than decorum.

Do whatever you need to do to get out.

When Assault Happens

This needs to be said plainly and carefully.

If you are sexually assaulted:

- It is not your fault
- It does not matter what you wore
- It does not matter what you drank
- It does not matter what you agreed to earlier
- It does not matter how well you knew them
- It does not matter if you froze
- It does not matter if you didn't fight

Responsibility belongs **entirely** to the person who chose to assault you.

What to Do After Sexual Assault

If you can, and when you are able:

- Go to a hospital or emergency room

- Or go to Planned Parenthood or a sexual assault clinic

- Ask for a **rape kit** (also called a sexual assault forensic exam)

You do not have to decide right away whether to report.

A rape kit can:

- Preserve evidence

- Document injuries

- Provide medical care

- Give you options later

You are allowed to take time to decide what comes next.

Reporting Is Your Choice

You may choose to:

- Call the police

- File a report later

- Never file a report

All of these choices are valid.

No one else gets to decide for you.

Medical care does **not** require reporting.

Support does **not** require reporting.

Healing does **not** require reporting.

If You Can't Do Anything Right Away

Sometimes the first thing people do is nothing.

They go home.
They sleep.
They dissociate.
They tell no one.

That is not failure.

That is survival.

You can still seek care later.
You can still talk to someone later.
You can still make choices later.

There is no expiration date on support.

Why This Chapter Exists

This book talks a lot about prevention.

But prevention does not always work.

That is not because someone failed.

It is because some people choose harm.

Talking about what to do when boundaries are ignored is not about fear.

It is about **having a path** when something goes wrong.

One Last Thing

If someone ignores your boundary once, they may ignore it again.

You do not owe second chances in situations involving your safety.

You do not owe explanations after harm.

You do not owe silence.

What you owe yourself is care.

What Comes Next

Next, we will talk about **aftercare**:

- What to expect emotionally
- Why reactions vary
- How to ask for support
- How to deal with self-blame
- How to begin healing

Because boundaries are allowed to protect you.

And when they fail, you are still allowed care, help, and dignity.

Always.

Aftercare and Counseling

After something violating happens, people often want to know *what they should feel.*

There is no correct answer.

Aftercare is not about doing recovery "right."
It is about **stabilizing, connecting, and being gentle with yourself** in the days and weeks that follow.

The First Thing to Know

What happened to you matters.

Your reaction — whatever it is — makes sense in context.

People respond to harm in many ways:

- Shock
- Numbness
- Anger
- Grief
- Fear
- Shame
- Confusion
- Relief that it's over
- A strange sense of normalcy

None of these reactions mean you're broken.
They mean your nervous system did what it needed to do to survive.

Trauma Is Not Just Memory — It's the Body

Trauma doesn't live only in thoughts.

It shows up as:

- Trouble sleeping
- Startling easily
- Feeling disconnected
- Difficulty concentrating
- Sudden waves of emotion
- Avoidance
- Physical tension
- Exhaustion

These are not signs of weakness.

They are signs that your body is trying to protect you *after* the danger has passed.

Healing often starts with helping the body feel safe again — not by forcing insight, but by restoring steadiness.

Immediate Aftercare: Small, Grounding Things

In the early days, focus on basics.

You don't need to process everything.

You need:

- Food
- Water
- Rest
- Warmth
- Familiar routines
- One or two safe people

Grounding helps:

- Holding something solid
- Sitting with your feet on the floor
- Gentle movement
- Being around calm, ordinary life

You are not behind if all you can do is get through the day.

That *is* progress.

Telling Someone — Or Not

Many people feel pressure to "tell their story."

You are allowed to:

- Tell one person
- Tell no one
- Tell different people different amounts
- Change your mind

You do not owe anyone details.

Choose people who:

- Listen without interrogating
- Don't rush you to forgive or report
- Don't center their own feelings
- Believe you without debate

If someone responds poorly, that is not a reflection of your truth.

Counseling Is Support, Not a Verdict

Seeing a counselor does not mean:

- You're damaged
- You're overreacting
- You'll be in therapy forever

It means you want support processing something that exceeded normal coping.

A good counselor helps you:

- Regulate your nervous system
- Make sense of your reactions
- Reduce shame
- Rebuild trust in yourself
- Reclaim choice

You are allowed to interview therapists.
You are allowed to leave if it doesn't feel right.
You are allowed to go slowly.

What Good Counseling Feels Like

Healthy counseling:

- Does not rush disclosure

- Does not minimize what happened

- Does not push forgiveness

- Does not force confrontation

- Does not make you relive details unnecessarily

It helps you feel:

- More grounded

- Less alone

- More capable of choice

- Less defined by what happened

Healing is not erasing memory.
It is restoring **agency**.

Faith, Meaning, and Care (If This Matters to You)

Some people want spiritual support.
Some need distance from it.

Both are valid.

If faith is part of your life, aftercare may involve:

- Being reminded that harm was not your fault

- Reclaiming your body as good

- Separating God from what was done to you

- Letting anger exist without guilt

If faith feels complicated right now, that is okay.

You do not need to resolve meaning to heal.

Common Traps to Avoid

Be gentle with yourself around these:

- **"I should be over this by now."**
  Healing is not linear.

- **"Others had it worse."**
  Pain does not compete.

- **"I should have known."**
  Responsibility belongs to the person who chose harm.

- **"If I think about it, I'll make it worse."**
  Avoidance can protect at first — processing can come later.

There is no timetable you're failing to meet.

Rebuilding Trust — Slowly

After trauma, trust often returns in stages:

- Trust in your own perceptions
- Trust in your boundaries
- Trust in selected people
- Trust in environments
- Trust in intimacy (if and when you choose)

You don't owe anyone access while you heal.

Boundaries remain your allies here.

One Important Truth

Needing help does not mean boundaries failed.

Boundaries are not guarantees.
They are supports.

When harm happens, the right response is not self-criticism
— it is **care**.

If You Are Reading This for Someone Else

If you are supporting someone who has been harmed:

- Believe them
- Listen more than you speak
- Avoid fixing
- Respect their pace
- Stay present over time

Consistency heals more than advice.

Moving Forward

Aftercare is not about returning to who you were before.

It is about becoming someone who knows:

- What safety feels like
- What support looks like
- That your body is not the enemy
- That your boundaries matter
- That healing is possible

It takes time.

And you do not have to do it alone.

"Stacy's Mom Has Got It Goin' On" —

and Stacy's Mom Is Not Flirting Back

Teenagers get crushes on adults.

This is normal.

It happens because teenagers are:

- Learning what attraction feels like
- Drawn to confidence and stability
- Curious about adulthood
- Practicing admiration before intimacy

A crush is not a plan.
It is not an invitation.
It is not consent.

It is part of growing up.

The question that matters is not *why teens have crushes.*

The question is **what adults do next**.

What a Healthy Adult Understands Immediately

A healthy adult recognizes three things right away:

1. **The attention is about development, not desire**
2. **The responsibility is entirely theirs**
3. **The correct response is not engagement, but containment**

They do not feel flattered.
They do not feel tempted.
They do not feel confused.

They feel **clear**.

Acknowledging Without Encouraging

Healthy adults do not pretend nothing is happening.

They also do not make it special.

They may:

- Respond politely
- Keep interactions brief
- Maintain normal tone
- Stay in public settings
- Redirect attention naturally

They do **not**:

- Tease
- Confide
- Joke about attraction
- Use flattery
- Create private moments
- Comment on appearance
- Suggest maturity beyond age

The adult does not need to say:

"I know you like me."

They simply behave in a way that makes engagement impossible.

Why "Just Being Nice" Is Not Enough

Some adults believe that as long as they don't *act* on attraction, they are behaving appropriately.

That is not true.

Boundaries are not just about behavior — they are about **signals**.

A healthy adult:

- Does not linger

- Does not reward attention with closeness

- Does not become the "cool adult"

- Does not invite emotional intimacy

- Does not blur roles

They understand that **attention itself can escalate** if it is fed.

So they don't feed it.

How a Healthy Adult Redirects

A healthy adult gently moves the interaction back where it belongs.

They:

- Talk about school, sports, or group activities
- Involve other adults
- Keep conversations task-focused
- Avoid personal disclosures
- End interactions cleanly

They are warm — but not inviting.
Kind — but not personal.
Present — but not available.

This is not rejection.

This is **care**.

The Adult Does Not Need to Be "Understood"

This matters:

A healthy adult does **not** need the teen to understand why nothing will happen.

They do not explain.
They do not justify.
They do not process feelings together.

They know that *explaining* often becomes engagement.

Instead, they let consistency do the work.

Boundaries teach without discussion.

The Adult Protects the Teen From Embarrassment

A healthy adult does not:

- Call attention to the crush
- Joke about it with others
- Shame the teen
- Make it public
- Turn it into a story

They protect the teen's dignity.

The goal is not correction.

The goal is **allowing the crush to pass without harm.**

Because it almost always does.

This Is What Safety Looks Like

When an adult handles this appropriately:

- The teen is not isolated

- The teen is not encouraged

- The teen is not confused

- The teen is not ashamed

- The teen is not pulled into secrecy

Time does the rest.

The crush fades.
The teen grows.
Nothing bad happens.

That is success.

Why This Chapter Comes First

Before we talk about predators, it's important to be clear:

Most adults who receive attention from teens do not act on it.

They don't struggle heroically.
They don't flirt accidentally.
They don't feel conflicted.

They simply **do not engage**.

That is the baseline.

Anything else is a choice.

A Line That Never Moves

Healthy adults know this without debate:

Teenagers are neighbors.
Teenagers are not partners.
Teenagers are not peers.
Teenagers are not confidants.
Teenagers are not responsible for adult feelings.

The adult's role is to **hold the boundary without drama**.

That is what love looks like when power is involved.

What Comes Next

Now that we've seen what appropriate adult behavior looks like, we can talk about the contrast.

Next, we will talk about:

- Adults who **notice the crush and lean into it**
- Adults who **reinterpret admiration as desire**
- Adults who **frame restraint as mutual struggle**
- Adults who **shift responsibility onto the teen**

In other words:
how predators behave differently — and why those differences matter.

Because boundaries don't just protect teens.

They expose intent.

And intent is revealed in what adults do **when they could do nothing at all**.

What a "Cool Adult" Actually Does

The phrase "cool adult" gets misused.

Sometimes it's used to describe an adult who bends rules, keeps secrets, or feels special to kids.

That's not a cool adult.

That's an unsafe one.

A genuinely cool adult looks very different.

A Cool Adult Is Cool to *Everyone*

A healthy adult is not selectively warm.

They are:

- Supportive to many people
- Consistent across ages
- Predictable in tone
- The same in public and private

They don't single one teenager out for special attention.
They don't create favorites.
They don't cultivate exclusivity.

If their warmth depends on secrecy, it's not warmth.

A Cool Adult Lives in Public Space

You'll notice where safe adults spend their time.

They:

- Show up to events
- Stay where others are
- Leave when events end
- Don't linger for "just one more conversation"
- Don't seek quiet corners or side rooms

They are present — not hovering.

They don't need privacy to connect.

A Cool Adult Talks About *Ideas*, Not Intimacy

Healthy adults are interesting without being intimate.

They can talk — in public — about:

- Politics
- World events
- Books
- Art
- Music
- History
- Science
- Philosophy
- Shared hobbies

These conversations are:

- Engaging
- Thoughtful
- Appropriate
- Non-personal

They do **not** talk about:

- Sexual topics
- Relationship problems
- Personal loneliness
- Attraction

- Body commentary

- "You're mature for your age"

Depth is not the same as intimacy.

A cool adult knows the difference.

A Cool Adult Is Not Looking for Emotional Supply

This matters.

Safe adults do not use teenagers to:

- Feel understood
- Feel admired
- Feel exciting
- Feel young
- Feel important
- Process adult problems

They have peers for that.

Teenagers are not emotional support animals.

A Cool Adult Does Not Seek Privacy

This is one of the clearest signs.

A healthy adult does not:

- Ask to be alone with a teen
- Invite private conversations
- Move interactions off-platform
- Suggest secrecy "so people don't misunderstand"
- Create "special" moments away from others

They don't need it.

Connection that requires privacy is not age-appropriate connection.

A Cool Adult Does Not Touch Other People's Children

This should not be controversial.

Safe adults:

- Do not initiate physical contact
- Do not hug unless clearly appropriate and welcomed
- Do not touch shoulders, backs, waists, or hair
- Do not play physical games that blur boundaries
- Do not "accidentally" touch

They let children and teens set the distance.

And they respect it immediately.

A Cool Adult Respects Roles

They don't blur lines.

They don't act like:

- A peer
- A confidant
- A secret-keeper
- A co-conspirator
- A replacement parent

They stay in their lane — comfortably.

They don't complain about boundaries.

They don't resent oversight.

They don't frame structure as unfair.

A Cool Adult Makes Safety Boring

This is the quiet truth.

Safe adults are often:

- Predictable
- Slightly boring
- Consistent
- Unremarkable in the best way

They don't create drama.
They don't generate intensity.
They don't thrive on attention.

And that's why they're safe.

Why This Matters

Predators often try to look "cool."

But what they're really doing is:

- Creating exclusivity
- Seeking validation
- Manufacturing intimacy
- Testing secrecy
- Blurring roles

Once you know what a real cool adult looks like, the difference becomes obvious.

The Litmus Test

Here's a simple question:

Would this adult's behavior still make sense if every interaction were fully visible to parents and other adults?

If the answer is yes — consistently — that's a good sign.

If the answer depends on privacy, secrecy, or special status, it's not.

Cool Adults Don't Need to Be Defended

One last thing.

Healthy adults don't require:

- Justifications

- Explanations

- "You don't understand them"

- Excuses

- Silence

Their behavior speaks for itself.

That's what safety looks like.

What Comes Next

Now that we've defined what *appropriate* adult behavior looks like, we can talk about the contrast:

- Adults who **test boundaries**
- Adults who **reframe attention**
- Adults who **seek secrecy**
- Adults who **shift responsibility**

In other words — how predators behave.

Because clarity is protective.

And boundaries don't just keep people safe.

They make intent visible.

One Rule for Kids:

Do Not Send Photos to Adults. Ever.

There is one rule that matters more than almost any other.

It is simple.
It is clear.
It has no exceptions.

Do not send photos to an adult.
Period.
Ever.

This Rule Is Not Complicated

You do not need to decide:

- If the adult is "nice"
- If you trust them
- If they asked politely
- If they said it was just between you
- If they promised not to share it
- If they said it was for a good reason

The answer is always **no**.

Why This Rule Exists

Adults do not need photos from children.

They do not need them for:

- Friendship
- Support
- Advice
- Mentoring
- Coaching
- Caring
- Curiosity
- "Just checking in"

Any adult who asks a child for photos is **crossing a line that exists to protect children.**

That line is not blurry.
It is not cultural.
It is not negotiable.

Responsibility Always Goes One Way

This matters:

If an adult asks a child for photos, **the adult is at fault**.

Not:

- Because the child misunderstood
- Because the child was curious
- Because the child agreed
- Because the child sent something first
- Because the child "looked older"

Children are not responsible for adult behavior.

Ever.

Adults Know This Rule

Safe adults already know this.

They do not ask.
They do not hint.
They do not joke.
They do not test.
They do not "accidentally" cross into this territory.

If an adult asks for photos, they are not confused.

They are **violating a boundary on purpose**.

What About "Legitimate" Photos?

If there is a legitimate reason for a photo to exist, one of these things is true:

- It was taken in public
- A parent was present
- A parent knows about it
- It was shared parent-to-parent
- It was taken by the adult's own child
- It was shown in a group setting
- It was part of an event or activity with adults around

Legitimate situations **never require secrecy**.

They never require private messaging.
They never require deleting messages.
They never require "don't tell."

Secrecy Is the Warning Sign

An adult who asks for photos often adds:

- "Just between us"
- "Don't make it weird"
- "Your parents don't need to know"
- "This is normal"
- "I won't save it"
- "You can trust me"

These are not reassurances.

They are red flags.

Safe adults don't need secrecy to do safe things.

If an Adult Asks, That Is Serious

This cannot be softened.

If an adult asks a child for photos:

- That adult is breaking the law
- That adult knows better
- That adult is unsafe
- That adult belongs nowhere near children

This is not about misunderstanding.

It is about **exploitation**.

What a Child Should Do

If an adult asks you for photos:

- Do not send anything
- Stop responding
- Tell a trusted adult
- Show them the messages
- Do not delete anything

You will not get in trouble.

You are not "making a big deal."
You are not ruining someone's life.
You are protecting yourself — and others.

What Adults Must Say Clearly

This rule should be stated plainly by parents, caregivers, teachers, and mentors:

"No adult should ever ask you for photos.
If that happens, tell me immediately."

Children should not have to figure this out on their own.

Why This Rule Is Non-Negotiable

This rule exists because:

- Photos can be used to manipulate

- Photos can be shared forever

- Photos create leverage

- Photos create fear and silence

- Photos shift power sharply toward the adult

No amount of trust makes this safe.

No amount of reassurance changes the risk.

One Rule Is Enough

Children don't need a long list.

They need one clear line:

No photos to adults. Ever.

Anything that tries to move that line is unsafe.

And when lines are clear, children are safer — because they don't have to negotiate.

They just have to say no.

If a Child Sends a Photo Unsolicited

This situation needs to be addressed plainly, because predators often try to confuse it on purpose.

Sometimes, a child sends a photo without being asked.

This does **not** change the rules.

The Rule Does Not Reverse

If a child sends a photo to an adult:

- The adult is still responsible
- The adult must still stop immediately
- The adult must not engage
- The adult must not keep the photo
- The adult must not respond privately

Consent does not travel upward.

A child cannot make an unsafe situation safe by initiating it.

What a Safe Adult Does Immediately

A safe adult responds in **one way only**:

They shut it down.

That means:

- No compliments
- No curiosity
- No questions
- No reassurance that it's "okay"
- No continued conversation

The response is brief, clear, and final.

Something like:

"I can't receive photos. You need to talk to your parent."

And then the interaction ends.

What a Safe Adult Does Next

After stopping the interaction, a safe adult takes responsibility for transparency.

They:

- Inform the child's parent or guardian
- Inform a supervisor if one exists
- Preserve evidence if required by law
- Remove themselves from further contact

They do **not**:

- Try to handle it privately
- "Protect" the child by hiding it
- Protect themselves by deleting records
- Continue contact "to make sure they're okay"

Safety requires other adults.

Why Any Other Response Is Unsafe

Predators often claim:

- "They sent it first"
- "I didn't ask"
- "I was trying to help"
- "I didn't want to embarrass them"
- "I didn't want to get them in trouble"

These are excuses.

A safe adult understands:

- Children experiment
- Children seek validation
- Children make mistakes
- Children misjudge attention

That is **why adults exist**.

The adult's job is to stop the situation — not manage it secretly.

The Child Is Not in Trouble

This matters deeply.

A child who sends a photo:

- Is not a criminal
- Is not "bad"
- Is not ruined
- Is not responsible for adult behavior

They need:

- Protection
- Education
- Support
- Boundaries
- Reassurance

Shame creates silence.

Silence protects predators.

Why Immediate Transparency Matters

Handling this privately creates danger.

Secrecy:

- Teaches the child that this is a shared secret
- Makes escalation easier
- Protects the wrong person
- Normalizes inappropriate contact

Transparency:

- Restores safety
- Brings in accountability
- Stops grooming immediately
- Protects future children

Safe adults choose transparency — even when it's uncomfortable.

"But What If the Adult Panics?"

This is not about feelings.

Fear of:

- Getting in trouble
- Being misunderstood
- Embarrassment
- Awkward conversations

does not override responsibility.

Adults are expected to handle hard situations appropriately.

That is part of being an adult.

One Sentence That Clarifies Everything

Here is the simplest test:

If an adult's response to a child's photo is anything other than stopping and reporting, that adult is unsafe.

There are no soft exceptions.

What Parents Should Tell Children

Children should be told clearly:

"If you ever send a photo to an adult and feel scared or confused, tell me.
You are not in trouble."

This gives children a way out — even after a mistake.

Why This Chapter Exists

Predators rely on confusion.

They blur responsibility.
They flip the story.
They claim innocence through passivity.

This chapter removes that confusion.

Adults are always responsible.

Children are always protected.

One Last Time, Clearly

- Children should not send photos to adults

- If they do, adults must stop and report

- Secrecy is never safety

- Transparency is protection

- Responsibility never belongs to the child

Boundaries do not disappear when someone makes a mistake.

They matter **more**.

When There Is No "Conflict" at All

Sometimes people imagine abuse as a story of temptation.

They picture an adult who feels torn.
Conflicted.
Struggling.
Resisting.

That story is comforting — because it suggests that harm only happens when lines get blurry.

But that story is often wrong.

Some Harm Is Not About Confusion

There are cases where:

- The adult does not feel conflicted
- The adult does not feel unsure
- The adult does not feel tempted and resist
- The adult simply wants something

There is no internal struggle.

There is only intent.

In those cases, the adult is not "caught off guard" by a crush.
They are not misreading signals.
They are not slowly sliding down a slope.

They are choosing.

The Myth of the "Special" Child

It's important to say this plainly.

Children are not seducing adults.

"Stacy's Mom" is not a song about an adult chasing children.

It is a song about children having a fantasy — and about adults not caring about being considered attractive by children.

That distinction matters.

Children:

- Are not sophisticated manipulators

- Are not offering adult desire

- Are not capable of mutual consent with adults

Admiration, attention, and crushes are developmental — not sexual agency.

When an adult harms a child, it is not because the child was irresistible.

It is because the adult decided to take advantage of power.

This Is Why Individual Morality Is Not Enough

Because not all harm comes from confusion, **personal virtue alone is not sufficient protection.**

This is where institutions matter.

Schools.
Churches.
Sports programs.
Camps.
Youth organizations.
Families.

Safety cannot rely on:

- "We trust our people"

- "They're good guys"

- "They've never caused problems"

- "They're respected"

- "They're famous"

- "They're charismatic"

Predators often rely on exactly that trust.

It Wouldn't Matter If It Were Brad Pitt

This is a useful thought experiment.

It doesn't matter if the adult is:

- Famous

- Attractive

- Charismatic

- Powerful

- Beloved

- Respected

- Wealthy

A safe adult — even one universally admired — would not entertain a child's attention.

Ever.

They would not flirt.
They would not joke.
They would not "handle it privately."
They would not test boundaries.

And a **safe institution would never allow the opportunity in the first place**.

Institutional Safety Is About Removing Opportunity

When predators act without conflict, the only effective protection is **structure**.

That means:

- No private access
- No unmonitored communication
- No one-on-one isolation
- No secrecy
- No exceptions "just this once"
- No reliance on reputation

Safety is not about reading minds.

It is about **closing doors**.

Other Adults Are the Boundary

One of the strongest protections for children is not rules — it is **other adults.**

Adults who:

- Are present
- Are attentive
- Are empowered to intervene
- Share responsibility
- Ask questions
- Document concerns
- Escalate issues without fear

Abuse thrives in silence.

It withers under shared oversight.

When Institutions Fail, It's Often Predictable

When abuse happens in institutions, it is rarely because no one knew.

It is because:

- Concerns were minimized
- Behavior was excused
- Access was protected
- Reputation mattered more than safety
- Reporting was discouraged
- "We don't want trouble" prevailed

These are not accidents.

They are choices.

Fixing Holes Is Not an Accusation

Good institutions assume **someone eventually will try.**

Not because people are bad — but because power attracts misuse.

So they:

- Audit communication channels
- Limit private access
- Rotate supervision
- Require transparency
- Train adults to intervene
- Document boundary crossings
- Fix weaknesses proactively

This is not distrust.

This is stewardship.

Safety Is a System, Not a Feeling

A child is safest when:

- No single adult has unchecked access

- No one is irreplaceable

- No one is above rules

- No one's word outweighs structure

- No one handles concerns alone

When systems work, predators don't need to be identified.

They are **blocked**.

Why This Chapter Matters

Talking about predators only as "conflicted" adults:

- Centers adult feelings

- Minimizes intent

- Obscures responsibility

- Blames victims implicitly

- Leaves systems unchanged

Talking about **structure** changes outcomes.

The Real Line

Here is the line institutions must hold:

No adult — no matter how admired —
is entitled to private, undocumented access to a child.

Ever.

Not for mentoring.
Not for care.
Not for discipline.
Not for talent.
Not for affection.

If access exists, it must be visible.
If a hole exists, it must be fixed.

This Is How Children Are Actually Protected

Not by hoping adults behave well.

But by ensuring:

- They don't have the chance to behave badly
- And can't hide if they do

That is not cynicism.

That is care.

When Two Adults Are Not on the Same Page

Not all harm happens because someone is underage.
Not all harm happens because someone intended to
manipulate.
Not all harm happens because someone broke a law.

Sometimes harm happens because **two adults are
standing in the same relationship but inhabiting
completely different meanings of it.**

This is one of the most common, least discussed, and most
poorly handled boundary failures in churches and faith
communities.

Legal Adulthood Is Not the Same as Shared Understanding

When people hear "two adults," they often assume symmetry.

They assume:

- equal awareness

- equal framing

- equal expectation

- equal power

But adulthood by age does not guarantee adulthood in **relational clarity**.

Two people can be legally adults and still be profoundly unequal in how they understand:

- what the relationship is

- what it has been

- what it might become

- what is at stake if it changes

In these situations, the problem is not attraction itself. The problem is **who introduces sexual or romantic meaning — and when**.

When a Relationship Changes Without Consent

Many relationships begin in a clearly non-sexual frame:

- mentor and mentee
- older and younger friend
- spiritual guide and seeker
- teacher and student
- caregiver and cared-for
- "safe adult" and emerging adult

These relationships are defined not by romance, but by **trust**.

Trust that:

- affection is not a prelude
- attention is not an invitation
- care is not conditional
- closeness is not a test

When one person later introduces sexual or romantic intent, the relationship does not simply "add a new option."

It **rewrites the past**.

Suddenly, the other person is forced to ask:

- *Was I misreading all of this?*
- *Was I being evaluated without knowing it?*
- *Was my trust a mistake?*

This is why the moment of revelation can feel shocking, even violent — not because sex was mentioned, but because **the category collapsed.**

What was safe is no longer safe.
What was grounding is no longer neutral.
What was freely given now feels retrospectively exposed.

That loss matters.

Responsibility Follows the Introduction of Meaning

In situations like this, responsibility does not belong equally.

It belongs to **the person who sexualized the relationship.**

Not because desire is evil.
Not because attraction is shameful.
But because introducing sexual meaning changes the terms of the relationship in a way that **cannot be undone.**

The person who trusted did not consent to that change.

And consent is not only about actions.
It is about **frames.**

You do not get to reframe a relationship and then ask the other person to adjust gracefully.

"I Didn't Mean It That Way" Is Not Repair

Often, the person who introduced sexual intent is genuinely confused by the reaction.

They may say:

- "I was just being honest."

- "I didn't mean anything by it."

- "I thought we were close enough."

- "I assumed you knew."

What these statements reveal is not malice.
They reveal **self-focus**.

They center:

- the speaker's feelings

- the speaker's clarity

- the speaker's relief

And they bypass the central truth:

The harm is not that desire existed.
The harm is that trust was altered without consent.

Intent does not undo that.

When Confusion Is the Harm

In many non-criminal scenarios, the harm is not pressure, coercion, or persistence.

The harm is **confusion.**

Confusion that forces someone to:

- reinterpret memories
- doubt their own perception
- question their instincts
- grieve a relationship they didn't know they were about to lose

This kind of harm is often minimized because it doesn't look dramatic.

But confusion erodes safety just as surely as pressure does.

A relationship that once steadied someone now destabilizes them.

That matters.

Can the Relationship Be Repaired?

Sometimes, yes.
Often, no.

Repair is **not automatic**, and it is **never owed**.

Whether repair is possible depends almost entirely on what the person who introduced sexual meaning does next.

Not what they feel.
Not what they hope.
Not how embarrassed they are.

What they do.

What Repentance Looks Like in Non-Criminal Harm

In situations like this, repentance is not theatrical.
It is not spiritualized.
It is not self-protective.

It looks like this:

1. **Immediate apology**
   No explanations. No qualifiers. No reframing.
   Just: *"I'm sorry. I crossed a boundary."*

2. **Naming the harm accurately**
   "I sexualized something that was safe. That was wrong."

3. **Owning responsibility without centering shame**
   "This is on me. I misread the relationship."

4. **Affirming the value of what was lost**
   "What we had mattered. I damaged it."

5. **Releasing control over outcome**
   "You don't owe me forgiveness, clarity, or continued relationship."

There is no timeline attached.
There is no request for reassurance.
There is no appeal to shared history.

Repentance does not ask to be understood.
It accepts consequence.

217

Forgiveness Does Not Require Restoration

In Christian communities especially, it must be said clearly:

Forgiveness does not require:

- continued access

- restored closeness

- emotional labor

- reconciliation

Forgiveness may mean:

- releasing resentment

- letting go of revenge

- wishing the other person well from a distance

A person can forgive and still choose **never to re-enter the relationship**.

That choice is not bitterness.
It is wisdom.

The Theology of Non-Possessive Love

Here the Church has something essential to offer — if it remembers its own theology.

Jesus tells us plainly:

In the resurrection, people neither marry nor are given in marriage.

That is not a detail.
It is a correction.

It tells us that:

- intimacy is not owned
- relationship is not secured through possession
- love is not validated by exclusivity

If we cannot imagine deep, lifelong, meaningful relationships that are **not sexual or marital**, we have already distorted love.

Christian love is not:

- escalation
- capture
- entitlement
- "what comes next"

It is:

- presence without claim
- affection without demand
- connection without possession

219

When someone introduces sexual meaning into a relationship that was not built for it, repentance means **learning to desire without grasping**.

That discipline matters — not just for safety, but for faithfulness.

When Repair Is Not Possible

Sometimes, even perfect repentance cannot restore what was lost.

That does not mean repentance failed.
It means reality is being honored.

In those cases, the faithful response is:

- distance
- restraint
- respect for loss
- refusal to reinsert oneself

Letting go is sometimes the most moral act available.

Why This Matters for Churches

Churches often mishandle these situations by:

- minimizing the harm
- pressuring forgiveness
- privileging the older or more established person
- treating confusion as oversensitivity

That compounds the damage.

A community that understands boundary responsibility will instead say:

- *The person who reframed the relationship bears the weight.*
- *Repair, if possible, happens on the harmed person's terms.*
- *No one is owed access simply because no crime occurred.*

That clarity protects everyone.

This Is Adult Work

Children do not need to navigate this.
Teenagers do not need to analyze this.
Young adults should not be asked to carry this complexity alone.

This is **adult moral labor**.

Adults must learn to:

- recognize asymmetry
- restrain desire
- repair without entitlement
- love without possession

So that younger people can experience relationships that are:

- clear
- boring
- predictable
- safe

Which is exactly what love looks like when power is handled well.

Repentance, Repair, and the Possibility of Non-Possessive Relationship

There are relationships that carry extraordinary weight.

You show up.
You listen.
You help.
You notice.
You protect.
You care deeply about whether the other person is okay.

From the inside, it can feel like marriage.

But it isn't.

It's not sexual.
It's not exclusive.
It's not possessive.
And it is not headed toward "more."

In Christian language, this is not confusion.
It is **ordinary faithfulness**.

You are your brother's keeper.
You are your sister's keeper.

That level of care is not exceptional — it is expected.

When Care Gets Mistaken for Claim

One of the most common adult failures is confusing *depth* with *entitlement*.

You can:

- care intensely
- feel responsible
- be emotionally invested
- share long history
- hold significant trust

And still have **no claim** on the other person's body, future, or reciprocity.

Christian love does not promise possession.

But when someone quietly converts care into desire — and desire into hope — a dangerous illusion forms:

After all this, surely this means something more.

That is where repentance becomes necessary.

Not because caring was wrong.
But because **claim was introduced where none existed.**

Repentance Is Not Regrouping

In non-criminal boundary failures, people often confuse repentance with strategy.

They think repentance means:

- apologizing
- stepping back briefly
- feeling bad
- waiting
- hoping forgiveness will "reset" the relationship

This is not repentance.

This is **regrouping**

Regrouping says:

I'll give them space now so I can try again later.

That posture makes restoration impossible.

Because it proves the boundary was never accepted — only paused.

Repentance Requires the Death of the Outcome

True repentance begins when you relinquish the outcome you wanted.

Not temporarily.
Not theatrically.
Completely.

That includes relinquishing:

- the hope of romance

- the hope of being "chosen later"

- the hope that forgiveness equals access

- the hope that patience will be rewarded

As long as someone is secretly holding onto:

Maybe someday, if they heal...

they are not repentant.

They are waiting.

And waiting is not safe.

Your Brain Is Not Neutral Ground

This matters enough to say plainly:

Your brain can be a **dirty, awful scratch pad of stupid.**

Thoughts form.
Fantasies attach.
Narratives develop.
Justifications multiply.

None of that makes you uniquely bad.
It makes you human.

But repentance requires you to stop treating your internal world as harmless.

What you rehearse internally shapes:

- what you notice

- what you hope for

- what you say "accidentally"

- what you push for subtly

You cannot claim repentance while privately nurturing desire you know cannot be honored.

That is not integrity.
That is rehearsal.

Fix the Interior — Don't Just Police the Exterior

Many people attempt repentance by controlling behavior alone.

They:

- stop texting as much
- avoid certain topics
- stay technically appropriate
- act restrained in public

But if the internal narrative remains unchanged, pressure leaks out.

Repentance requires **interior correction**.

That means:

- confronting fantasy instead of indulging it
- refusing mental rehearsal
- interrupting entitlement when it appears
- grieving the loss honestly rather than spiritualizing it

You don't fix the relationship first.

You fix **yourself**.

Control Your Mouth and Your Actions

While that interior work is happening, something very practical is required:

You control your mouth.
You control your actions.

That includes:

- not "checking in" emotionally

- not seeking reassurance

- not fishing for warmth

- not explaining yourself again

- not hinting at regret or longing

- not sharing how hard this is for you

Repentance does not need to be witnessed repeatedly.

One clear apology is sufficient.

After that, restraint is the proof.

Restoration Is Not a Right

This must be said clearly, especially in Christian contexts:

Restoration is not guaranteed.
Restoration is not owed.
Restoration is not proof that repentance "worked."

Sometimes the most faithful outcome is **distance**.

Sometimes the relationship cannot be safely re-entered without reopening confusion.

Sometimes the cost of restoration would fall entirely on the person who was harmed.

In those cases, insisting on restoration becomes another form of selfishness.

Letting go is not failure.
It is obedience.

Forgiveness Is Not the Same as Access

Forgiveness may happen internally.

Forgiveness may mean:

- releasing resentment

- refusing revenge

- wishing the other person well

Forgiveness does *not* mean:

- resuming closeness

- restoring intimacy

- sharing emotional space

- continuing the relationship

Forgiveness can coexist with permanent boundary.

Anyone who demands access in the name of forgiveness has not understood forgiveness at all.

The Discipline of Non-Possessive Love

Here the Christian tradition speaks with unusual clarity — if we listen.

Jesus teaches that in the resurrection, people do not marry.

That is not a dismissal of marriage.
It is a **reorientation of love**.

It tells us that:

- relationship is not secured by exclusivity

- love does not depend on possession

- intimacy does not require ownership

Christian love is meant to train us in **non-possessive attachment**.

To love deeply without claiming.
To care without capturing.
To be faithful without demanding return.

If you cannot love someone without needing them to belong to you in some way, love has already turned inward.

When Repair *Is* Possible

Sometimes, after real repentance, a relationship can be restored — but only under strict conditions:

- The person who crossed the boundary does not lead the repair

- The harmed person sets pace, distance, and form

- Sexual or romantic framing is permanently removed

- There is no private emotional intensity

- There is no revisiting "what might have been"

Even then, restoration often looks **smaller** than before.

Less intense.
Less frequent.
More public.
More structured.

That is not loss.
That is wisdom.

When Repair Is Not Possible — and That Is Enough

Sometimes repair never comes.

The relationship ends.
Contact stops.
Silence remains.

This is not a spiritual tragedy.

It may be the most honest outcome available.

The faithful response then is not despair — it is transformation.

You take what you learned about:

- entitlement
- desire
- fantasy
- restraint
- responsibility

and you become safer for others.

That is fruit.

This Is the Work Adults Must Do

Children do not need to carry this complexity.
Teenagers should not be asked to manage it.
Young adults should not be responsible for correcting it.

This is **adult moral work**.

It requires:

- honesty about desire

- discipline of thought

- restraint of action

- surrender of outcome

- acceptance of loss

When adults do this work well, children experience
something simple:

Care without confusion.
Attention without pressure.
Love without cost.

Which is exactly what love is supposed to look like.

There Is No "Yeah, Yeah, Yeah — We Know"

Why We Have to Talk to the Kids Every Year

There is a phrase people use when they are tired of hearing something they believe they already understand.

"Yeah, yeah, yeah. We know."

It sounds like confidence.
It sounds like familiarity.
It sounds like maturity.

But in this case, it is simply false.

Because it keeps happening.

Children are still harmed.
Teens are still targeted.
Trust is still exploited.
Adults are still surprised.
Churches are still saying, *"We never thought it would be him."*

So no — we do not "know."

Not in the way that matters.

Familiarity Is Not Formation

One of the great mistakes adults make is confusing *having heard something before* with *having been formed by it.*

Churches hear about abuse:

- when a scandal breaks
- when a survivor speaks
- when a headline circulates

They respond with:

- a meeting
- a policy update
- a training
- a statement

And then, slowly, the urgency fades.

The conversation becomes background noise.

"Yeah, yeah, yeah. We know."

But knowing facts is not the same as practicing vigilance.
Agreement is not the same as transformation.
And policies are not the same as culture.

Formation requires repetition.

The Problem Is Not That Children Forget

It's That Adults Do

Children are not the ones who drift toward complacency.

Adults are.

Adults:

- assume good intentions are enough
- trust familiarity more than structure
- resist inconvenience
- grow tired of constraints
- forget why boundaries exist
- resent oversight once urgency fades

Adults relax first.

And when adults relax, children pay the price.

That is why this book has spent so much time on **adult responsibility**.

Because children are not failing to protect themselves.

They are doing exactly what children are supposed to do:

- trusting
- attaching
- learning
- admiring
- depending

The question is whether adults remain worthy of that trust.

Why This Has to Be Annual

We talk to children every year not because children are forgetful —
but because **new children arrive every year.**

Every year:

- children age into new spaces

- teens enter new developmental stages

- authority figures change

- volunteers rotate

- leaders come and go

- social dynamics shift

A one-time conversation assumes a static world.

Churches are not static.
Children are not static.
Risk is not static.

Annual repetition is not paranoia.
It is stewardship.

Why Children Don't Need the Whole Story

Children do not need:

- adult psychology

- sexual dynamics

- abuse typologies

- stories of worst-case scenarios

- detailed explanations of grooming

Giving them that would be inappropriate — and irresponsible.

Children are not meant to manage adult failure.

That is why this entire book exists **before** the children's guide.

Adults need the full complexity so children don't have to carry it.

Children need:

- clear expectations

- simple rules

- predictable adults

- visible boundaries

- repeated reassurance

- multiple safe paths to help

Not once.
Every year.

Simplicity Requires Adult Discipline

What we say to children must be simple.

But simplicity is not easy.

Simplicity requires:

- adults who have done their own work
- adults who are not defensive
- adults who are not minimizing
- adults who are not improvising
- adults who agree on the message

You cannot speak simply to children if adults are confused, divided, or uncomfortable.

You cannot repeat a message yearly if you don't actually believe it.

That is why this guidebook exists.

Repetition Is How Safety Becomes Normal

Children learn what matters by what is repeated.

We repeat:

- prayers
- songs
- rituals
- stories
- seasons

Because repetition forms identity.

When children hear the same safety message every year, from multiple adults, in consistent language, something important happens:

Safety becomes ordinary.

Not dramatic.
Not scary.
Not secret.

Just normal.

And when safety is normal, harm stands out.

What Annual Conversations Do (Quietly)

Talking to children every year:

- reminds them which adults are safe
- reminds them that boundaries are expected
- reminds them that secrets are not required
- reminds them that help is always allowed
- reminds them they are not alone

It also does something equally important:

It reminds adults that children are watching.

That accountability matters.
That trust is fragile.
That access is a responsibility, not a reward.

This Is Not About Fear

It Is About Faithfulness

We do not talk to children every year because the world is terrifying.

We talk to them because love is active.

Because keeping requires attention.
Because care requires structure.
Because faithfulness requires memory.

And because silence has never kept children safe.

What Comes Next

The next section of this work is not smaller because it is less important.

It is smaller because it is **clearer**.

It will not explain everything.
It will repeat a few things well.
It will use simple language.
It will sound familiar year after year.

That is intentional.

Children do not need new information annually.
They need **consistent truth**.

Adults need depth.
Children need clarity.

So now that we have done the adult work —
now that we have named responsibility, power, boundaries, repair, and restraint —

we can speak to children in a way that is calm, honest, and steady.

Every year.

Because there is no "yeah, yeah, yeah, we know."

Not while it keeps happening.
Not while children are still growing.
Not while we are still responsible.

And we are.

www.ingramcontent.com/pod-product-compliance
Lightning Source LLC
Chambersburg PA
CBHW060415130626
46555CB00005B/2080